Wreaths

make it in
Minutes

Wreaths

TAYLOR HAGERTY

LARK BOOKS

A Division of Sterling Publishing Co., Inc.
New York / London

Book Editor
Catherine Risling

Copy Editors
Lecia Monsen
Ashlea Scaglione

Photographer
Zachary Williams
Williams Visual

Stylist
Brittany Aardema

Book Designer
Kehoe+Kehoe Design
Associates

A Red Lips 4 Courage Communications, Inc., book
www.redlips4courage.com
Eileen Cannon Paulin
President

Catherine Risling
Director of Editorial

Library of Congress Cataloging-in-Publication Data

Hagerty, Taylor.
    Make it in minutes. Wreaths / Taylor Hagerty. -- 1st ed.
        p. cm. -- (Make it in minutes)
    Includes index.
    ISBN-13: 978-1-60059-317-8 (HC-PLC with concealed spiral : alk. paper)
    ISBN-10: 1-60059-317-8 (HC-PLC with concealed spiral : alk. paper)
    1. Wreaths. I. Title. II. Title: Wreaths.
    TT899.75.H34 2008
    745.92'6--dc22

                                        2007046348

10 9 8 7 6 5 4 3 2 1

First Edition

Published by Lark Books, A Division of
Sterling Publishing Co., Inc.
387 Park Avenue South, New York, N.Y. 10016

Text © 2008, Taylor Hagerty
Photography © 2008, Red Lips 4 Courage Communications, Inc.
Illustrations © 2008, Red Lips 4 Courage Communications, Inc.

Distributed in Canada by Sterling Publishing,
c/o Canadian Manda Group, 165 Dufferin Street
Toronto, Ontario, Canada M6K 3H6

Distributed in the United Kingdom by GMC Distribution Services,
Castle Place, 166 High Street, Lewes, East Sussex, England BN7 1XU

Distributed in Australia by Capricorn Link (Australia) Pty Ltd.,
P.O. Box 704, Windsor, NSW 2756 Australia

If you have questions or comments about this book, please contact:
Lark Books
67 Broadway
Asheville, NC 28801
(828) 253-0467

Manufactured in China

ISBN 13: 978-1-60059-317-8

For information about custom editions, special sales, premium and corporate
purchases, please contact Sterling Special Sales Department at (800) 805-5489
or specialsales@sterlingpub.com.

"Symbolizing eternal hope, the wreath goes 'round and 'round, and where it starts or ends cannot be found. Woven of things that grow— for life, and hung for holiday delight."
—Unknown

Contents

Introduction

Wreaths have an ancient history, stretching back to the original Olympic games in Rome when olive and laurel branches were woven into circlets and placed on the heads of victors. While it's not known exactly when the wreath made the transition from head to wall, it's not a stretch to imagine that those athletes saved their trophies by hanging them on the walls of their homes.

Through the years the wreath has come to be enjoyed for many reasons, from marking the change of seasons to celebrating special holidays to adding the finishing touch to a home's decor. Here you'll find projects that use traditional elements and forms, as well as those that challenge tradition by using clever materials and shapes. Unleash your creativity with the help of these basic techniques and make a wreath to tempt a baker, please a new mother, warm a home, or charm a special child.

CHAPTER 1

Every craft has tools, materials, and techniques that make projects come together quickly and easily, allowing you to showcase your creative flair. The first thing to do when designing a wreath is to determine its theme. That decision will guide you in choosing the type of base and embellishments. When it comes to bases, you can always choose from traditional shapes and materials; however, using something unique, such as flip-flop sandals or a wooden frame, ratchets up the uniqueness quotient from the everyday to truly spectacular. Learn how to tie an impressive bow or make your own wreath bases using grapevine, foam, or a simple wire hanger. Once you've mastered these techniques, you're well on your way to designing distinctive wreaths for any occasion.

Embellishments

Buttons
Buttons have come a long way from the basic round shape. They are available at craft and fabric stores in themed novelty sets and large-quantity assortment bags. Adhere with glue dots, hot glue, strong-hold glue, or craft glue.

Fabric
With a nearly unlimited variety of textures, weights, and colors, fabric is a multipurpose element in wreath design. Use airy tulle to tie an ethereal bow or wrap the base in denim for a casual, masculine touch.

Flowers, plants, and herbs
Traditionally, some sort of plant material is used when making a wreath. Everything from evergreen branches to herbs to flowers and even lowly weeds has graced the curve of a wreath.

Found items
Practically everyone has a stockpile of everyday items such as costume jewelry, stray game pieces, unused keys, and mismatched spoons. They can be an untapped resource for unique wreaths.

Glitter
Glitter is available in a rainbow of colors with sheer and opaque qualities. Textures range from ultra fine to chunky grains to snowflake-like drifts of mica. A solid bond is ensured by using double-sided tape, glitter glue, or adhesive paper. A fine tip for glitter glue is essential for detailed work.

Memorabilia
Anything that reminds you of a special occasion, whether it is photos, souvenirs, ticket stubs, or coins from a foreign country, can make a sentimental wreath project. Create a wreath using greeting cards for a milestone birthday or favorite holiday.

Natural items

Creating an organic wreath is easy to do using natural elements such as bamboo pieces, a bird's nest, birdseed, realistic plastic or foam eggs, feathers, moss, or pinecones. When using these materials it's a good idea to display the wreath in a protected spot, because it won't withstand buffeting by the elements.

Raffia

Raffia is a natural material made of strips from a large palm tree that are cut and dried. The resulting fibers are a natural creamy brown that can be dyed different colors. It can withstand some moisture but if it's been dyed, it will likely bleed on the surrounding area.

Ribbon

Available in a mind-boggling variety of widths, colors, and materials, there is surely a perfect ribbon for every type of wreath. It is important to choose good-quality ribbon for your projects—nothing can ruin a wreath more quickly than sub-par ribbon.

Seashells

Seashells make wonderful embellishments on any nautical-themed wreath. Shells can be used as subtle accents or clustered with ornaments, ideal for holiday décor.

Twine

Twine is composed of two or more strands of yarn, cotton, sisal, jute, or hemp twisted together to create a strong string. It's usually a neutral tan color but is also available in many colors. Twine is a great substitute for ribbon in natural or country-style designs.

Yarn

In addition to its use as wrapping for a wreath base, yarn is a textural choice for both the eyes and the fingers. It is found in a wide variety of colors, thicknesses, styles, and materials. Tied into a bow or gathered into bunches, yarn is an uncommon accent on a wreath.

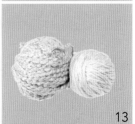

Adhesives

Craft glue
This thick, versatile adhesive can be applied with a foam brush and will hold heavy embellishments securely in place. It does take some time to dry and form a bond, so take that into account as you are choosing adhesive for a wreath project.

Double-sided tape
This convenient tape works best for paper-to-paper adhesion. It is simple to use and creates a quick, permanent bond.

Floral tape
This tape is a strong, stretchy, non-sticky material that is ideal for securing floral wire to the stems of silk or fresh flowers, reinforcing weak stems while simultaneously hiding the wire.

Hot glue gun and glue sticks
This adhesive is used for most projects in this book. It works quickly and is quite strong on most surfaces. It is available in two forms: high-temp (hot) glue and low-temp glue. High-temp glue melts at a high temperature and is best for bonding ceramics, metal, plastics, wood, or other non-porous materials or heavy items. In general, the higher the melt temperature of the glue, the stronger the bond created. Low-temp glue melts at a lower temperature and cools quickly. Use it on lightweight embellishments and when applying adhesive directly to polystyrene foam forms. (High-temp glue will melt most foam.)

Permanent adhesive
Permanent adhesive is sold in a squeeze tube and bonds a wide variety of surfaces including glass, metal, and plastic.

Spray adhesive
Spray adhesive comes in a spray can and is used to quickly cover surfaces with a light misting of glue. Use it when covering a polystyrene form with potpourri, berries, or petals. This product dries very quickly, so work fast.

Materials

Floral pins
These pins work well to secure materials to foam shapes. Pins are available in a variety of shapes and sizes. The most common sizes are the longer corsage pins that range between 2"–2½". The shorter boutonniere pins are usually between 1¼"–2" long.

Floral spray paint
An easy way to integrate a wreath base into your color scheme is to use spray paint. Available in a wide range of colors and finishes, spray paint is fast and dries fairly quickly. Choose an interior-exterior paint for durability. Use multiple light coats instead of one or two heavy ones to avoid a runny, drippy mess.

Foam core board
This useful, lightweight board is made by adhering heavy paper to both sides of a thin foam core. Available at most craft stores in many colors, thicknesses, and sizes, foam core board is great for making unusually shaped bases and for reinforcing paper elements such as signs and photos.

Moss
Used to cover floral foam and arrangement mechanics. Popular varieties include Spanish moss in natural or green, sheet moss, and reindeer moss. All achieve coverage; choice depends on personal preference and design style.

Polystyrene foam
Available in green or white and has a very course texture. Polystyrene foam comes in sheets and preformed shapes such as spheres, cones, and wreaths.

Wire
Wire is very important for sturdy design. It is available in a variety of gauges ranging from #16 to #28; the smaller the number of wire, the larger gauge thickness. Wire can be purchased in precut lengths of 12" or on a roll. Rolled wire is called paddle or reel wire. It is used in wreath-making when one continuous strand is needed for stability.

Tools

Craft knife

Craft scissors

Floral snips or shears

Foam brushes

Measuring tape

Needle-nose pliers

Polyurethane spray

Ruler

Sandpaper

Serrated knife

Wire cutters

Wired floral picks

Wreath Bases

The foundation of a wreath supports both the elements of the wreath and the theme of the design. It can be made using traditional bases, which range from polystyrene foam to twigs, vines, or wire and are available in most craft stores. For a more unusual base, consider using flip-flop sandals, a lariat, or jump rope.

Foam
Foam wreath bases are best used with floral or other lightweight embellishments and are available in green injection-molded and white polystyrene as well as floral foam. The injection-molded foam base is difficult to insert materials into without first piercing a hole in the foam. White polystyrene foam is easy to work with and works best if embellishments are hot glued to the form. Floral foam is specifically designed for use with fresh flowers and greens. It is usually soaked in water until it is thoroughly saturated and then decorated.

Natural materials
Bases made from flexible vines, willow, twig, straw, and grains such as broomcorn are wonderful bases for nature-inspired wreaths. Grapevine and willow-type bases tend to be sturdier and will withstand the elements in a sheltered location. They can also support heavier embellishments. Straw, twig, and grains generally require the additional support of a wire base.

Wire
These pre-formed bases made of several rows of wire provide a uniform shape. Wire bases are good for delicate dried flowers but can also handle heavyweight embellishments. A basic wire base formed using a coat hanger is a simple, inexpensive alternative, but it doesn't offer a lot of support, so you'll need to use lightweight materials for embellishment.

Wood
A wooden frame with wide edges makes for an unusual wreath. Decoupage paper onto the frame or wrap it with strips of fabric. To add bulky softness, first wrap strips of batting around the frame and then cover with strips of fabric. Another unusual type of wooden form is a large embroidery hoop. These are made from balsa wood and are available in a variety of sizes.

time-saving tip

Making Interesting Wreaths
Unconventional shapes such as rectangles, ovals, squares, or even giant monograms are an interesting twist. Consider making very small or very large wreaths for different effects. Use three smaller embellished wreaths strung together to form a wreath garland.

Techniques

Hanging a wreath

When you're ready to display your creation, you can always use a nail; however, this creates a hole in your door or wall. Instead, there are a wide variety of hangers on the market. Some use a plastic hook and removable adhesive, others feature a molded over-the-door arm with a hook, and some employ magnets.

Each product will have a recommended weight limit to help you choose the correct type for your wreath. You can make your own wreath hanger using a plain wire coat hanger. Straighten the hanger and then bend it to fit over your door so you can hang the wreath on the hook.

Making a foam core base

Create your own foam base by drawing the desired shape on a piece of foam core board and then cutting it out with a craft knife. To add bulk, simply adhere polystyrene foam blocks to the foam core shape using a low-temp glue gun. Use a paring or serrated knife to shape the blocks if necessary. You can also use heavy-duty cardboard in place of foam core board.

Making a grapevine wreath

To make a grapevine wreath, soak several long vines in a large tub of water until they are flexible. Remove the vines from the water and trim leaves and unnecessary twigs with floral shears as desired. *Note:* Use fresh vines to skip the soaking.

Coil the vine into approximately the finished size you want, weaving any excess vine into the coil. Continue to weave additional vines, starting in a different spot on the wreath, until you've reached the thickness you want. *Note:* Secure the vines in spots with twists of floral wire to maintain the shape of the wreath.

Because the wreath was soaked, or if you used fresh-cut vines, you'll need to allow the wreath to dry. Leave it outside in the sun for a few days or bring it inside and hang it. If you hang the wreath, you'll need to rotate it periodically to maintain its shape. To accelerate the drying time, place the wreath in an oven set at 170 degrees F (76.6 C) or lower and watch it carefully for approximately 30–40 minutes. If the wreath begins to warp out of shape, place it between two oven racks to flatten.

Making a simple wire base

You can make a simple wire base using a wire coat hanger. Form the hanger into the shape you want—a circle or heart shape is your best bet. Leave the hook attached to use as a hanger or cut it off in the middle of the twist using wire cutters. Bend the cut ends down the wreath shape.

Shaping hairpin wires

Hairpins are used to pin moss and foliage into foam. They are easily made if "S" pins are not available or a smaller discreet pin is needed in the design. Using wire cutters, cut 20- or 22-gauge wire into 2" segments. Bend at center and fold wire into equal parts to create hairpin.

Storing a wreath

There comes a time, particularly with seasonal wreaths, when you'll want to store your wreaths. Proper packaging will ensure that the wreath emerges next season in flawless condition, ready to be displayed. There are plastic and fabric wreath bags available for purchase that will protect their contents from dust, insects, and fading, but you can also use inexpensive large black plastic drawstring bags. Place the wreath in the bag so the drawstring is at the bottom and then pierce a hole in the seam of the bag and thread a large hook through to hang it. Pull the drawstring tight and knot. Other options include specially made cardboard wreath boxes that will allow you to store the wreath lying down instead of hanging it. Of course, a regular cardboard packing box in the appropriate size will work just as well.

Taping wire

Begin covering wire by wrapping floral tape around the top of the wire, stretching tape slightly and using your thumb and index finger to twist the tape around the wire. Work down the wire, gently stretching the tape with one hand as you twist the tape down the wire with your thumb and index finger of your other hand. Pinch off tape at the end of the wire.

Tying a simple bow

Make one loop at each end of a ribbon length, being careful not to twist or bunch the ribbon. Cross the right loop over the left, wrapping the right loop behind the left, then under, and up through the hole. Pull the loops into a smooth knot. Adjust the loops and trim the tails so they are slightly longer than the loops.

The bow may be attached directly to the project with hot glue or attached with floral wire.

Using a Bow-Making Tool

Bow-making tools were invented to hold looped ribbon in place, leaving your hands free to secure the bow with wire. They also make it easy to get creative with your floral bows by adding a variety of different ribbons and even strings of pearls, greenery, feathers, and flowers. They are fairly inexpensive, but if you love to use ribbon, consider creating your own.

Materials

- ▨ Craft knife
- ▨ Foam core board (2' square)
- ▨ Pencil
- ▨ Ruler
- ▨ Wire

Instructions

1. Measure, mark, and cut 4" line in one side of foam core board using craft knife (Fig. 1). Make slit wide enough to hold several folds of ribbon.

2. Follow directions for making a Florist Bow, but instead of holding loops with fingers, simply slide ribbon loops into cut (Fig. 2).

3. When you are done, carefully pull out layered bow and twist wire around middle of loops to secure.

Fig. 1

Fig. 2

Making a florist bow

Fig. 1

Fig. 2

Fig. 3

Pinch the ribbon and form a loop, leaving desired length of ribbon for one bow tail (Fig. 1). Make same-size loop in the opposite direction (Fig. 2).

Continue adding loops on each side, securing them under thumb and forefinger, decreasing loop lengths for each layer (Fig. 3).

Fig. 4

Fig. 5

Once you have desired number of loops, twist one last small loop around your thumb to make center loop (Fig. 4). Insert floral wire through center loop and twist tightly on bow back, securing all loops. Fluff out bow, starting with bottom two loops.

Pull loops tightly in opposite directions. Continue with remaining loops until you have desired bow shape (Fig. 5). Trim tails to desired length using an angled cut. To create a forked cut, fold end of ribbon in half lengthwise and cut at an angle toward folded edge.

time-saving tip

Discreet Restraint

Small dabs of hot glue can be applied to ribbon loops or tails and discreetly attached to the wreath form to hold the desired shape.

CHAPTER 2

There are special occasions to celebrate throughout the entire year. This chapter contains wreaths to honor mom on Mother's Day and a heart-shaped offering for Valentine's Day. Create a touching circlet to commemorate the birthday of a loved one or the union of a special couple. If someone you know has achieved a milestone, fashion a wreath proclaiming it's time to celebrate. Hang the Halloween bell wreath on your front door to add the perfect touch to spooky decor, and it will even scare the hobgoblins away whenever the door is opened or closed. A wreath is a unique way to highlight a special day, proclaiming to those who pass by that there is a momentous occasion to be celebrated.

Vintage Santa

Materials

- 8" x 10" oval mirror
- 8" x 10" wooden base
- Adhesives: permanent adhesive, spray adhesive
- Artificial bird
- Christmas card
- Craft scissors
- Decoupage medium
- Embossing powder: clear
- Feathers: black, white (6 each)
- Flowers: fabric (6–8)
- Glitter: clear glass
- Sandpaper
- Scrapbook paper
- Stars (3 large, 5 small)
- Tinsel: silver
- Velvet leaves (6)
- Wreath: small gold pine

Instructions

1. Tear scrapbook paper and collage around Christmas card image. Adhere to wood base using decoupage medium; let dry thoroughly.

2. While collage is drying, sand portions of silver backing off mirror until you achieve the look you want.

3. Spray artificial bird, flowers, and velvet leaves with adhesive. Sprinkle on glitter; let dry.

4. When collage is dry, glue mirror over top of collaged wood base with permanent adhesive.

Easy Removal

Lightly wetting the sandpaper will take the silver backing off of the mirror more quickly.

Holiday greetings are rubber stamped on the front of the image using clear ink that is set with clear embossing powder.

Adding Glitz

Adding sparkle to embellishments creates a timeless winter accent to holiday wreaths. There are many ways to glitter objects, depending on the effect you want. For a heavier look that resembles snow, generously dip the area in white glue. Globs and drips will collect large amounts of glitter that will have depth and texture when dry. For a light, sprinkled look, use a paintbrush to apply a small amount of glitter adhesive. Be stingy, because everywhere the adhesive is, you will end up with permanent glitter.

Left: The cluster of embellishments hides the wooden base of the Vintage Santa wreath. **Right:** Everything from the artificial bird to the flowers and leaves is glittered.

5. Adhere tinsel around perimeter of wreath, securing in place with permanent adhesive.

6. Cut individual branches from gold wreath; adhere around outside of wreath along with feathers, velvet leaves, flowers, jingle bells, glittered stars, and artificial bird.

7. Stamp holiday greeting on front of mirror; set with embossing powder.

time-saving tip

Applying Glitter

When applying the glitter, work over a large piece of cardstock with a fold down the middle. Sprinkle the glitter over the adhesive on the object you are working with. When finished, gently pickup the paper by each side and coax the extra glitter to the fold in the middle of the cardstock. The glitter will line up along the fold, and can be gently tipped back into the bottle for future use.

Winter Wonderland

Materials

- 14" foam wreath
- Clear glass bulbs: large (24), medium (20), small (24)
- Craft scissors
- Floral wire
- Hot glue gun and glue sticks: low-temp
- Iridescent shreds (3 bags)
- Pencil or skewer
- Ribbon: 3" wire-edge
- Wire cutters

Instructions

1. Remove ornament hangers from all glass bulbs. Fill bulbs with iridescent shreds.

2. Apply hot glue to opening of ornament; press firmly into foam wreath. Repeat to cover wreath. *Note:* Begin with the largest bulbs around the outside edge and work toward the inside of the wreath.

3. Hot glue medium and small bulbs in place. *Note:* Some bulbs will be hot glued to other ornaments instead of onto the foam.

4. Fill in gaps with loose shreds to cover any exposed foam.

5. Tie 3 yards of ribbon into large bow; attach to top of wreath with floral wire and trim ends.

time-saving tip

Here's a Little Help

Use a pencil or bamboo skewer to help push the iridescent shreds into the narrow opening of the clear glass bulbs.

Happy Birthday

Materials

- ½" circle punch
- 14" wicker wreath
- Acrylic paint: blue, green, pink, purple, white, yellow
- Birthday candles (about 24)
- Cardstock: assorted scraps, pink, white
- Chipboard scraps
- Curling ribbon: blue, green, pink, white
- Die-cut balloons (6)
- Fine-point marker: black
- Floral wire: white
- Glue stick
- Greeting card: small
- Hot glue gun and glue sticks
- Party horns (6)
- Ruler
- Scissors: craft, decorative-edge
- Spray paint: white
- Tissue paper: blue, pink, yellow
- Wire cutters

Instructions

1. Spray paint wreath white; let dry. Wrap with curling ribbon.

2. Cut two 3" chipboard circles. Arrange candles in an arch on chipboard, with about ½" of candle base on chipboard; hot glue in place. Glue additional circle to top of candle base to stabilize.

3. Hot glue chipboard circles/candles to lower back of wreath.

4. Paint die-cut balloons with acrylic paint; let dry. Attach to floral wire with hot glue. Arrange balloons so at least one is touching top of wreath and hot glue in place. Hot glue remaining balloons to each other for stability and twist wire together at base. Attach to back of candle base with hot glue.

time-saving tip

Search and Remove

If you've used hot or low-temp glue in making your wreath, hold the finished project up to the light to remove the "strings" left from the glue gun.

Curling ribbon and tissue paper flowers add a festive touch to the Happy Birthday wreath.

5. Cut eight 6" circles from tissue paper with decorative-edge scissors. Twist center of each circle to form flower shape. Attach an equal number to each side of wreath and one behind candle arch. Add party horn to each side and glue on additional candles using hot glue.

6. Curl two 10" lengths of each curling ribbon with scissors. Adhere to lower center of wreath with hot glue.

7. Punch circles from assorted scraps of cardstock and adhere randomly on 2" x 3" piece of white cardstock with glue stick. Draw black lines to suggest strings.

8. Cut 2½" x 3½" piece of pink cardstock, adhere card with circle shapes, and tuck into wreath.

time-saving tip
Maintaining Balance

In wreath making, as in life, balance and scale are very important. Choose embellishments with the scale of the wreath in mind. While you're making and decorating your project, occasionally step back and view your wreath from a distance to ensure the elements are distributed evenly.

Valentine's Day

Materials

- ½"–¾" buttons (8)
- 4½" cookie cutter: heart-shaped
- Cardstock: coordinating prints (4)
- Craft knife
- Craft scissors
- Double-sided tape
- Embroidery floss: off-white
- Foam core board
- Foam dots
- Inkpad: brown
- Pencil
- Ruler

Instructions

1. Draw 14" circle with 12" circle centered inside foam core to create wreath; cut out with craft knife.

2. Cut 24 hearts, six from each print of cardstock, using cookie cutter as template.

3. Edge hearts with brown ink by rubbing edges directly on inkpad. Position 16 hearts on surface of foam core wreath; adhere with double-sided tape.

4. Layer eight hearts by attaching with foam dots on top of others.

5. Tie embroidery floss through buttons with small bows on top; adhere to center of each heart in top layer with double-sided tape.

6. Cover any exposed foam core with scraps of cardstock left over from heart cutouts.

time-saving tip

Die Cut Your Hearts

To speed up this project, use a heart die-cut machine instead of hand tracing and cutting out the hearts.

Wedding Cake Topper

Materials

- 12" foam wreath: white
- Bride and groom figure
- Craft scissors
- Decorative metal bowl: small
- Floral snips
- Forget-me-nots (1 bunch)
- Hot glue gun and glue sticks: low-temp
- Pearl–head corsage pins (2)
- Ribbon: 1" ivory satin
- Rub-on letters/words
- Ruler
- Silk lily-of-the-valley stem
- Silk roses (3)
- Stem pearls (2)
- Tulle: ivory
- White doves (2)
- Wire cutters
- Wire loop

Instructions

1. Cut tulle into 15"-long pieces (about 34–36 to completely cover wreath). Tie each piece into simple shoestring bows around wreath form. *Note:* Tie closely together to achieve fullness and completely cover the wreath.

2. Prepare metal bowl to become wreath base by gently pressing sides inward to flatten slightly. Hot glue bowl base to wreath.

3. Snip stems off roses using wire cutters and cluster where wreath meets metal base. Hot glue in place.

4. Hot glue bride and groom figure to inside center base of wreath.

time-saving tip

Customize Your Sentiment

The wreath banner can be personalized with the names of the bride and groom, the wedding date, or an apropos sentiment. There are many ways to add the wording, including using rubber stamps, computer-generated words, and paint pens.

A Christmas ornament makes an attractive and easy center for a cake topper wreath. It can be removed from the topper after the event and be a special holiday keepsake for years to come.

time-saving tip

Subtle Swathing

Wrap the wreath form in fabric, paper, or ribbon before applying embellishments to aid in adhesion and to prevent the form from showing through the decorations.

5. Snip stems off lily-of-the-valley and insert into wreath to highlight figures. Hot glue stems in place.

6. Cut satin ribbon to 15" length. Using rub-on letters, add desired sentiment.

7. Attach ribbon banner-style across top front of wreath, securing each end with corsage pin. Hot glue doves and forget-me-nots onto ends of banner.

8. Nestle large pearls randomly in tulle; hot glue in place.

9. Insert wire loop to hang directly into back of wreath; hot glue in place.

A decorative metal bowl with hearts turned upside down serves as the base of the Wedding Cake Topper wreath.

time-saving tip

Presto Chango

The Cake Topper wreath can be easily customized for other occasions. A stork or baby shoe ornament is perfect for a baby shower. A sparkling heart ornament would work well for an anniversary. Consider a favorite storybook or cartoon character for a child's birthday cake. Substitute candy or beads for the roses around the base for a less romantic celebration.

Halloween

Materials

- 14" jingle bells: large (52)
- Chipboard letters: B (1); O (2)
- Enamel spray paint: black, orange
- Glitter: orange
- Hot glue gun and glue sticks
- Ruler
- Spray adhesive
- Wire: heavy-gauge
- Wire cutters

Instructions

1. Form wire into 12" diameter. Bend back 1" of each end to create loops to connect ends.

2. Paint 26 jingle bells orange and 26 jingle bells black; let dry completely. *Note: Allow each coat to dry completely so there are no drip marks or paint blemishes.*

3. Slide jingle bells onto wire frame, alternating colors. When finished, snap wreath shut.

4. Apply spray adhesive to front of chipboard letters and sprinkle on glitter; let dry.

5. Attach letters to bottom of wreath with hot glue.

time-saving tip

Weathering the Elements

If the wreath is to be hung on an outside door, make sure that the embellishments will stand up to the elements.

Mother's Day

Materials

- Beads: acrylic leaf (2); filigree silver ball (3); Swarovski glass seed (20–30)
- Buttons: ecru (enough to cover wreath shape)
- Fabric glue
- Fabric marker or chalk
- Felt: cream
- Fusible web
- Inkpads: gold, stone
- Linen fabric
- Needle
- Paper flowers: small (2)
- Rubber stamps: alphabet letters
- Ruler
- Scrap paper
- Thread: ecru
- Wire craft hanger with clips: small

Instructions

1. Draw 5½" circle on front of 7" linen square using fabric marker or chalk. Draw another circle inside, about 2½" wide.

2. Sew buttons within the two circles, leaving a small space at lower right for embellishment. When sewing buttons, overlap some or balance others on top of each other. *Note:* It is fine to leave small gaps between button clusters.

3. Arrange silver ball and acrylic leaf beads and paper flowers in a pleasing manner; attach using fabric glue. Fill in as many gaps as you prefer with glass seed beads using fabric glue.

4. Using 7" square of fusible web, attach finished linen square to 8" square of cream felt.

5. Cut tiny piece of paper to fit within the hanger's frame opening, then stamp MOM in gold and stone.

6. Hang completed wreath from the clips on hanger.

Holly Laurel

Materials

- Beading wire: gold
- Craft scissors
- Flocked pinecones (3)
- Floral tape
- Floral wire
- Gemstones: red (16)
- Hot glue gun and glue sticks
- Ribbon: 2" red satin
- Ruler
- Velvet leaves (2 stems)
- Wire cutters

Instructions

1. Place two velvet leaves with stem ends overlapping at center (leaves facing opposite). Allow 6" space between bottom leaf of each stem.

2. Wrap 6" length of wire around center of two bare stems. Finish with floral tape to secure and hide wire wrap. *Note:* Use floral tape that matches the color of the stems.

3. Bend stem of each leaf to form horseshoe shape.

4. Using gold beading wire and red gemstones, form "springy" stems of jeweled holly berries. Hot glue red gemstone on one end of spring and wrap other end around leaf stem.

5. Tie 1 yard of ribbon into bow and wire securely to center of bare stem.

6. Wrap 12" length of floral wire around each pinecone. Wire pinecones to wreath.

time-saving tip

Don't Forget to Flock

No flocked pinecones? Use a small paintbrush to add thinned white craft glue to natural pinecones and sprinkle them with green, white, or iridescent glitter.

CHAPTER 3

A wreath embellished with flowers, herbs, or fruits will tantalize the senses both visually and by its aroma. The projects in this chapter are perfect housewarming gifts and are a wonderful way to use the bounty of your garden to decorate your home. They recall the renewal of spring, the warm days of summer, and an abundant fall harvest deep in the heart of winter when all that is green and growing lies dormant. Inspired by nature, one project featuring a variety of succulent plants and some bamboo evokes a Zen-like tranquility. Let go of any preconceived notions of what "must" be on a wreath and allow your imagination to discover new ways to use everyday plants.

Bay Leaves

Materials

- 10" foam wreath
- Bay leaves: 2 oz.
- Craft scissors
- Faux red chilies: wire stems (8–10)
- Hot glue gun and glue sticks: low-temp
- Ribbon: 2" wire-edge
- Ruler

Instructions

1. Hot glue stem end of bay leaves to wreath form, overlapping leaves shingle-style.

2. Tie 2 yards of ribbon into florist bow; tie to wreath and trim ends at an angle.

3. Hot glue wire stems of chilies onto bow.

time-saving tip

Fast & Cool Hot Glue

Pressing the bay leaves into hot glue with a cold table knife will cool the hot glue quickly.

Rosebuds

Materials

- 10" foam wreath
- Craft scissors
- Floral pin
- Hot glue gun and sticks: low-temp
- Ribbon: 1" wire-edge
- Rosebuds: paper (200)
- Wire cutters

Instructions

1. Cut stem wire of rosebuds to about 1" using wire cutters.

2. Completely cover wreath with rosebuds by dabbing small amount of hot glue on end of wire; insert into foam wreath.

3. Wrap long loop of ribbon around top of wreath; secure with floral pin or hot glue to backside. Tie simple bow on top of loop; adhere three rosebuds at center of bow.

time-saving tip

Perfect Your Pattern

Create a pleasing floral display by facing all of the rosebuds in the same direction.

Organic Succulent

Materials

- 15" moss-covered wreath
- Chicken and hen plant
- Dusty Miller plants (2)
- Faux bamboo
- Glass stones (5)
- Hot glue gun and glue sticks
- Jade plants (2)
- Lambs' ears (5)
- Moss-covered stones (3)
- Ruler
- Sedum plants (2)
- Wire cutters
- Wired wooden picks (12)

Instructions

1. Ready wreath form by securing any loose moss in place with hot glue.

2. Using wired wooden picks, lengthen stems of succulent plants as needed.
   Note: This will help ease the plants' insertion into the wreath.

3. Insert largest plants first, opposite one another for balance; hot glue in place.

4. Using smaller plants, create clusters and fill in wreath; hot glue in place. Add moss-covered stones to fill in empty spaces; hot glue in place.

5. Cut faux bamboo into two 15" segments using wire cutters. Adhere on top of wreath and hot glue in place.

6. Hot glue glass stones as accents among clustered plants, grouping stones for impact.

time-saving tip

Get Real

Use found rocks and stones for a realistic look. Gather other natural elements such as twigs, moss, and lichens for an organic feel. This wreath can be made with fresh succulents, too, as the plants are easily rooted in a moist moss.

Rosemary

Materials

- 12" wire wreath form
- Cheesecloth
- Craft scissors
- Dried cooking herbs
- Floral snips
- Fresh rosemary
- Paddle wire
- Raffia: green, orange
- Ruler
- Twine
- Wire cutters

Instructions

1. Snip rosemary into 5" segments and then gather 8–10 pieces into small bundles. Using short pieces of wire, wrap one end to secure. *Note:* You will need about 16–18 bundles to cover the 12" wreath.

2. Lay one bundle on wreath and secure by wrapping with wire twice.

3. Continue layering bundles to cover stem ends and wrapping each with wire to completely cover wreath.

4. Tie raffia in bow and wire to wreath form.

5. Create bouquet garni with 5" square pieces of cheesecloth filled with dried cooking herbs. Tie closed tightly with twine.

6. Tie bouquet garni onto wreath form and then tie raffia bow at center. *Note:* The bouquet garni can be snipped from the wreath as needed for cooking.

time-saving tip

Change Your Herbs

Create another gourmet kitchen wreath following the steps above using bay leaves or other wood-stemmed herbs such as oregano or thyme.

Dried Hydrangea

Materials

- 15" foam wreath: green
- Craft scissors
- Craft wire
- Dried hydrangea (20–22 heads)
- Floral snips
- Hot glue gun and glue sticks: low-temp
- Pearl tassel
- Pearls
- Polyurethane spray
- Ribbon: 2" green wire-edge
- Ruler
- Sheet moss: green
- Wire cutters
- Wired wooden picks

Instructions

1. Cover edges of foam wreath with green sheet moss; secure in place with hot glue.

2. Snip hydrangea heads into small clusters using floral snips, following natural stem breaks. Add wooden pick to each stem.

3. Insert hydrangea clusters into foam, snuggling one bundle against the next. Continue to fill and cover wreath.

4. Spray wreath with polyurethane to preserve hydrangea; let dry.

5. Hot glue pearls randomly into wreath to accent.

6. Tie 1 yard of ribbon into bow and trim ends; add pearl tassel at center with wire. Using wire, tie bow onto wreath base.

time-saving tip

Try a Different Shape

It's easy to create the look of the Dried Hydrangea wreath using other foam shapes such as an open heart, solid heart, or cross for a special holiday design.

Fragrant Lavender

Materials

- 12" x 15" wooden frame
- Craft scissors
- Dried lavender (1 bunch)
- Floral snips
- Hot glue gun and glue sticks
- Paddle wire

- Pepper grass (1 bunch)
- Ribbon: 1½" purple silk wired
- Ruler
- Silk wax flowers (4 stems)
- Wire cutters

Instructions

1. Divide lavender into small bundles of 15–16 stems. Gather stems and bind with short length of wire. Snip stems to about 4" in length. Continue creating bundles until you have about 16. Repeat with wax flowers and pepper grass.

2. Using wire, wrap free end around wooden frame twice at top corner. Lay one small bundle on top corner of frame and wrap wire twice around stems and frame.

3. Lay second lavender bundle on frame covering stems of first bundle; wrap stems twice with wire. *Note:* Do not cut the wire; use the continuous strand to complete this project.

4. Continue with remaining bundles to complete frame, alternating wax flowers and pepper grass between lavender bundles.

5. Cut ribbon into four 18" segments; tie each into a simple bow and trim ends.

6. Place one bow in each corner of wreath, securing in place with hot glue.

time-saving tip

Making Scents

To keep this fragrant lavender scent heady, add a small drop of lavender oil as needed to freshen.

Mini Pumpkins

Materials

- 3" miniature faux pumpkins (8)
- 18" twig wreath
- Clear polyurethane spray
- Hot glue gun and glue sticks

Instructions

1. Arrange pumpkins evenly around inside edge of twig wreath.

2. Adhere pumpkins in place with hot glue gun.

3. Spray entire wreath with polyurethane spray; let dry.

time-saving tip

Eye on the Base

A good pre-assembled wreath base can be found in a discount store, hidden under unattractive decorations. It's easy to remove poor-quality silks and plastic decorations and create your own wreath using the base.

Fall Glitz

Materials

- 18" grapevine wreath
- Artificial bird
- Coq feathers (5)
- Craft scissors
- Craft wire
- Curly willow: gold glittered (1 stem)
- Dried lotus pods (5)
- Floral snips
- Gilt persimmons (2)
- Hot glue gun and glue sticks
- Lucite silver dollars (1 stem)
- Magnolia leaf garland
- Preserved prunus leaves (1 stem)
- Ribbon: 1" brown wired
- Wire cutters

Instructions

1. Lay magnolia garland on grapevine wreath and wire in several places to secure. Tie bow with ribbon and attach to wreath with wire.

2. Bend stem of curly willow and insert among magnolia garland to accent. Secure in place using wire.

3. Snip Lucite silver dollar stem into three smaller pieces following natural joints of stems. Insert one segment into wreath at bow; secure in place with hot glue.

time-saving tip

Light up Your Table

Place a pillar candle in the center of the wreath for a fun candle ring centerpiece.

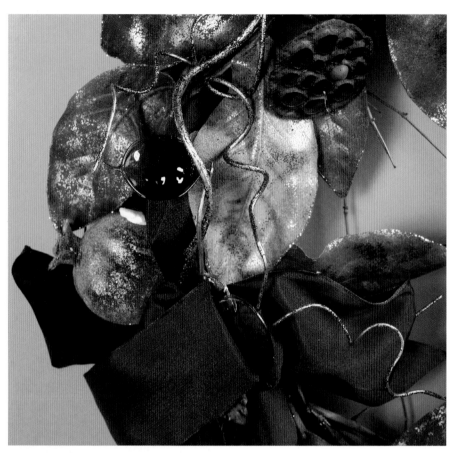

Gold gilded leaves, fruit, and curly willow gives the wreath a lustrous sheen. If you cannot find pieces already done, it is easy to add gold highlights yourself.

Gilding Fruit and Leaves

The art of gilding is ancient, and if done seriously requires several time-consuming steps as well as special handling of the gold leaf. Fortunately, there are several ways to quickly get a similar effect. One option is to use a dry foam craft brush and gold craft paint. Lightly touch the dry brush in a small dab of paint. Run the brush back and forth on a piece of paper to be sure there is only a small amount of paint and that the brush is fairly dry. Gently and lightly run the brush over the surface of the object. Once you have a feel for how the paint applies, you can dab gold highlights over the fruit or leaves.

A glittered bird with natural feathers nestled into the wreath is a nice focal point for the wreath. You can easily glitter a bird yourself with brush on craft paint with the sparkle in the blend. Small bottles of glitter paint are available in a wide variety of colors in craft stores.

4. Place lotus pods and persimmons among magnolia leaves for a natural look; secure in place with hot glue.

5. Insert remaining Lucite dollar stems to accent pods; secure in place with hot glue.

6. Using brown prunus leaves as needed, fill in garland for added fullness.

7. Hot glue three coq feathers to bird's tail. Snuggle bird into garland; hot glue in place. Using remaining feathers, highlight wreath and secure in place with hot glue.

time-saving tip

Wrap a Frame

Use floral or greenery garland for a quick cover on wreath frames—they are economical and easy to adhere.

CHAPTER 4

"A moment lasts all of a second, but the memory lives on forever." The projects in this chapter will help memories remain fresh in your mind. Feature a treasured collection of photos from a trip on a wreath bound with leather straps that suggest old-fashioned luggage. Celebrate the rite of back-to-school with a clever wreath featuring the tools of a student. An unforgettable party is commemorated with clusters of the corks from the night's empty wine bottles. The childhood freedom of lazy summer days is called to mind with brightly colored flip-flops topped off with pinwheels. There are even wreaths for the dog lovers and starfish collectors among us. Whatever the memory, there's a unique way to display it.

Family Heirlooms

Materials

- 14" square foam wreath
- Bookplate: large oval
- Cardstock: black
- Computer and printer (optional)
- Cosmetic sponge
- Craft glue
- Craft scissors
- Decorative paper: cream, vintage-themed
- Dried flowers (5–6)

- Family photos (10–12)
- Fine-point marker: black or brown
- Foam brush
- Hot glue gun and glue sticks: low-temp
- Inkpad: brown
- Keys: large skeleton (2)
- Photo corners: black (4 per photo)
- Raffia: natural

Instructions

1. Using craft glue and foam brush, cover wreath with torn pieces of vintage-themed decorative paper. Add antique look by lightly rubbing brown ink onto wreath's surface using cosmetic sponge.

2. Tie dried flowers and skeleton keys to lower side of square with raffia; reinforce with hot glue if necessary.

3. Computer print or hand-write family name on cream decorative paper to fit large bookplate. Mount to lower corner of wreath.

4. Mount photos on black cardstock, leaving about ⅛" border around photo. Place photo corners on all photos except ovals. Arrange and adhere photos to wreath with craft glue.

Back to School

Materials

- Bell with handle
- Chalk: white
- Chalkboard spray paint: black
- Craft glue
- Craft knife
- Craft scissors
- Crayons (about 100)
- Floral wire
- Foam core board
- Hot glue gun and glue sticks
- Pencil
- Ribbon: ½" ruler-themed
- Rickrack: ¾" black
- Ruler: 6" wooden
- Stars: gold (3)
- Wire cutters

Instructions

1. Draw 13" circle onto foam core. Draw 6" circle in center of larger circle; cut out with craft knife. Spray with chalkboard paint; repeat coat as necessary.

2. Adhere 2 yards of rickrack around inside and outer edges of wreath, overlapping cut edges with craft glue.

3. Break crayons in half. Adhere end with point to back of outside of wreath with tips extending beyond edge using hot glue. Hot glue flat end to extend beyond center of wreath. *Note:* It will take fewer crayons to fill the inside of the wreath than the outside.

4. Hot glue ruler and pencil to wreath. Tie 2 yards of ribbon into bow around handle of bell and attach to wreath with floral wire. Adhere gold stars and write simple math equation with chalk.

5. Create hanger with floral wire; hot glue to backside of wreath.

Family Dog

Materials

- 12" broomcorn wreath
- Clear polyurethane spray
- Craft wire
- Dog biscuits: large (10)
- Hot glue gun and glue sticks
- Raffia
- Rawhide puppy treats (9)
- Ribbon: 2" plaid
- Wire cutters

Instructions

1. Spray dog biscuits with two coats of polyurethane spray, front and back; let dry.

2. Adhere three sets of three puppy treats together with hot glue. Tie with raffia.

3. Place puppy treats equidistance on wreath, adding dog biscuits in between.

4. Tie 1 yard of ribbon into florist bow; attach to wreath with wire.

time-saving tip

Go for the Faux

Rather than using real dog biscuits and having to spray on polyurethane, keep your eye out for plastic bones that you can easily adhere with a strong-hold adhesive.

Wine Corks

Materials

- 12" wooden wreath frame
- Craft knife
- Craft scissors
- Dried baby's breath
- Dried "pistil-like" flowers
- Floral wire: thin
- Hot glue gun and glue sticks
- Ribbon: 3" coordinating (2)
- Silk leaves: large (30)
- Wine corks (about 30)
- Wire cutters

Instructions

1. Wrap wooden frame tightly with one of the ribbons, making sure it is secure. Hot glue ends in place at back of frame.

2. Arrange leaves around frame, securing in place with hot glue.

3. Bunch one flower and some of baby's breath together to make four groupings. Adhere around frame, evenly spacing and securing in place with hot glue.

4. Using craft knife, sharpen ends of corks to a point. Cut 15 of them in half length-wise.

5. Hot glue sharpened corks around groupings of flowers. Face points of corks inward, toward frame, with flat end sticking out toward you. Balance halved corks and whole corks in each group. *Note:* Using halved and whole corks gives the wreath more dimension.

6. Tie second ribbon in a big, floppy bow; trim ends at an angle. Wind wire through knot of bow and around frame tightly to secure in place.

Vacation Memories

Materials

- 16" grapevine wreath
- Craft scissors
- Hot glue gun and glue sticks
- Leather strip
- Memorabilia
- Mini-metal frame
- Postcards (4)
- Ruler

Instructions

1. Cut leather scraps into eight 1½"–2" strips. Wrap strips around wreath form; adhere with hot glue on backside.

2. Tuck various memorabilia under vines of wreath; secure in place with hot glue.

3. Create "luggage strap" hanger with 2"x18" strip of leather. Push section of leather into center of mini-metal frame and then tuck twigs from wreath under leather, extending over frame sides to form a faux buckle. Wrap around wreath, securing in place with hot glue.

4. Attach postcards to wreath with hot glue.

Summertime Flip-Flops

Materials

- Craft wire: silver #20
- Flip-flop clips (4)
- Flip-flops (8)
- Hot glue gun and glue sticks
- Pen or pencil
- Pinwheels (3)
- Straight pins (about 25)
- Wire cutters

Instructions

1. Arrange flip-flops by layering one on top of the other. Push a piece of craft wire from top flip-flop to bottom to hold in place.

2. Pull wire up outside of flip-flops and twist both ends to connect. Twist wire around pen or pencil to curl.

3. Using hot glue, add flip-flop clips for decoration. Attach pinwheels through flip-flops, securing in place with hot glue.

4. Push straight pins through back of flip-flops to hold shape.

Monogram Letter

Materials

- 12" wooden letter form
- Floral snips
- Hot glue gun and glue sticks
- Jeweled butterfly
- Polyurethane Spray
- Silk hydrangea bush

Instructions

1. Using floral snips, cut individual flower blossoms from silk hydrangea bush.

2. Hot glue individual flower blossoms to letter, clustering closely to cover completely. Use any remaining blooms to fill in open gaps.

3. Spray wreath with polyurethane to preserve hydrangea; let dry.

4. Hot glue jeweled butterfly at top of wreath to accent.

time-saving tip

Get into Shape

You can also use corrugated paper or polystyrene foam to form the letter base. Simply trace a letter template of your choice and cut to shape with a serrated knife. The form can be covered with ribbon or moss before adding flowers or greenery.

Starfish

Materials

- 12" grapevine wreath
- Coral or shell: small
- Dried starfish (4)
- Flower that resembles sea urchin: cream
- Hot glue gun and glue sticks
- Inkpads: black, soft sea colors
- Ornaments: small satin (12)
- Rubber stamps: alphabet
- Shipping tag
- Spray paint: white

Instructions

1. Lightly spray grapevine wreath white until it resembles driftwood.

2. While the wreath is drying, assemble shipping tag by stamping desired message, such as By the Sea, with alphabet stamps. For added interest, glue on a piece of coral or small shell by the hole where the string goes.

3. Attach flower in lower right portion of wreath with hot glue. Attach two starfish on either side of the flower in the same manner.

4. To imitate sea bubbles, remove hangers from ornaments and attach in a pleasing manner with hot glue.

5. Tie string of the tag to top middle of wreath so it dangles in center.

time-saving tip

Save Big

Discount and dollar stores are great sources for inexpensive ornaments for your wreaths.

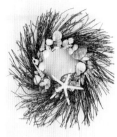

CHAPTER 5

So much of one's life can be found in the bits and pieces that accumulate as the days go by. Old game pieces, buttons from grandmother's button box, the odd group of silver spoons that has been passed through the generations, and even antique costume jewelry can come together to create distinctive wreaths to decorate your home or to give as gifts. Frequent the aisles of a discount store to find all sorts of interesting, inexpensive items to embellish a unique wreath. The most unlikely spots can provide inspiration for a wreath: gathering shells on the beach, digging through your grandmother's attic, or strolling through a flea market can yield surprising results.

Found Objects

Snowman

Materials

- 1" buttons: black (5)
- Craft foam: orange
- Craft knife
- Craft scissors
- Fleece: blue and white print
- Floral spray paint: white
- Floral wire: white #24
- Grapevine wreaths: 8" (1); 10" (2); 12" (2); 14" (1)
- Hot glue gun and glue sticks
- Scarf: red
- Spray snow flock
- Sticks: about 18" (2)
- Wire cutters

Instructions

1. **To create snowman form:** Place one 12" wreath inside 14" wreath and wire together. Place one 10" wreath inside one 12" wreath and wire together. Place 8" wreath inside 10" wreath and wire together. Wire 14" wreath (bottom of snowman) to 12" wreath (snowman body). Wire 10" wreath (snowman head) to 12" wreath.

2. Spray paint all wreaths white; let dry.

3. **To make the hat:** Fold 18"x15" piece of fleece in half, with seam vertical, approximately 8", to fit head. Hot glue together up seam. Fold cuff up from bottom. Tie piece of fleece at top approximately 3" from top of hat. Cut fleece at top in strips about ½" apart.

4. Cut out nose from orange craft foam using craft knife. Hot glue buttons and nose to snowman. Wrap scarf around neck and tie in place. Hot glue hat to head and sticks to sides of snowman body.

5. Spray wreath with snow flock; let dry.

Seashells

Materials

- Craft scissors
- Fish netting
- Hot glue gun and glue sticks
- Seashells: variety (about 60)
- Starfish

Instructions

1. Arrange seashells in center of wreath; hot glue in place.

2. Hot glue netting over a portion of the shells.

3. Intertwine starfish in netting; hot glue in place.

time-saving tip

Cover Your Tracks

Hide any visible hot glue holding the netting in place by covering it with a seashell.

Buttons & Bows

Materials

- 10" floral foam wreath
- Craft glue
- Craft scissors
- Decorative paper: variety
- Hot glue gun and glue sticks: low-temp
- Inkpads: coordinating colors (2–3)
- Markers: fine-tip black; medium-tip coordinating colors (3–4)
- Ribbon: 1", 3" coordinating colors
- Ruler
- Sandpaper: fine-grit
- Wooden disks: 1" (26); 1½" (22)

Instructions

1. Cut rough circles of decorative papers slightly larger than wooden disks. Adhere paper to disks with craft glue; let dry. Using sandpaper, sand away excess paper and smooth edges.

2. Apply ink to edges of disks by rubbing inkpad directly on all sides. Draw 2–4 small dots with assorted medium-tip markers in center of covered disks; accentuate and draw "threads" with black marker.

3. Wrap wreath with 3 yards of 3" ribbon to completely cover.

4. Hot glue "buttons" to cover top surface of wreath. Tie 2 yards of 1" ribbon into bow; trim ends.

Bling Bling

Materials

- 6"–8" foam wreath
- Costume jewelry: bracelets, brooches, earrings, necklaces
- Craft glue
- Craft scissors
- Hot glue gun and glue sticks: low-temp
- Lace ribbon
- Ruler

Instructions

1. Glue one end of 3' length of lace ribbon to back of frame.

2. Gently wrap lace ribbon around foam wreath to give a full, delicate look.

3. Glue other end of ribbon to back of frame.

4. Hot glue jewelry pieces on top of ribbon. *Note:* Do not take off the backs of the earrings and brooches as they give the wreath dimension.

5. Continue attaching pieces until the entire wreath is covered.

time-saving tip

Cluster as You Go

Use jewelry pieces that are vibrant and luminescent to give this wreath a fun, bright look. Feel free to have the pieces of jewelry overlap; clustering will make the wreath fuller and more interesting.

Starburst

Materials

- 12" foam wreath
- Hot glue gun and glue sticks: low-temp
- Leafing pen: silver
- Spray paint: silver, various shades of metallic (3)
- Wooden stars: $3/4$"–3" (100)

Instructions

1. Spray paint foam wreath silver. Spray a quarter of the larger stars with each shade of metallic paint. Edge all stars with silver leafing pen.

2. Insert one point of star into sides of foam wreath by coating tip with hot glue and pressing into foam; repeat with various sizes of stars and at different levels on inside and outside of wreath.

3. Hot glue stars onto top surface. Glue smaller stars on top of larger stars.

time-saving tip

Using Hot Glue

When using hot glue, be sure to keep a cool bowl of water nearby just in case the glue gets on your fingers. If this does happen, rinse immediately and peel off any remaining glue.

Circle of Spoons

Materials

- 6" corrugated wreath form
- Craft scissors
- Hot glue gun and glue sticks
- Ribbon: 2" black-and-white gingham wired; 3" toile paper
- Ruler
- Teaspoons (16)

Instructions

1. Wrap form with 3 yards of toile ribbon; hot glue ribbon ends to secure in place.

2. Evenly space eight of the teaspoons on wreath form with bowl of spoon pointing inward to center of form; hot glue each securely in place.

3. Place remaining eight spoons on wreath form between existing spoons with bowls of spoons pointing outward; hot glue each securely in place.

4. Hot glue 18" length of gingham ribbon to top of wreath to form loop for hanging.

5. Tie simple bow with remaining ribbon at top of loop to finish.

time-saving tip

Add More Ribbon

Dress up the Circle of Spoons wreath quickly by tying small bows of coordinating ribbon around every other spoon handle.

Vintage Junque

Materials

- 8" foam wreath
- Floral spray paint: dark brown
- Game tiles (about 30 small, 40 large)
- Metal flowers (15), leaves (8)
- Metal hand
- Permanent adhesive
- Typewriter keys (25)
- Vintage chandelier drop
- Vintage doll's head
- Vintage tinsel: dark gold

Instructions

1. Spray paint wreath form dark brown; let dry.

2. Adhere tinsel around inside and outside perimeter of wreath using permanent adhesive.

3. Using permanent adhesive, adhere game tiles, typewriter keys, and metal leaves and flowers.

4. Using permanent adhesive, adhere vintage doll's head, chandelier drop, and metal hand to finish wreath.

time-saving tip

Get Soaked

Achieve a rusty patina on the metal by soaking it overnight in equal parts plain vinegar and household bleach.

Peacock Feathers

Materials

- 15" vine branch wreath
- Coq feathers (8)
- Floral snips
- Hot glue gun and glue sticks
- Peacock feathers: tail (14); wing (18)

Instructions

1. Place peacock wing feathers in circular pattern following natural lines of wreath; hot glue to secure in place.

2. Trim peacock tail feathers using floral snips and insert into established pattern from Step 1.

3. Create depth by integrating coq feathers into pattern; hot glue to secure in place.

time-saving tip

Feather Alternatives

Use a pre-made coq feather wreath, adding vibrant peacock, pheasant, and ostrich feathers to accent. Also, a feather boa can also be wrapped around a polystyrene form to create an instant feather wreath.

CHAPTER 6

Hobbies make an interesting topic for wreaths. Christen an artist's studio with a wreath that holds the tools of his or her trade. Designate a cozy spot for knitting with a soft wreath that appears to have been fashioned from a sweater. Warm a kitchen with bundles of cinnamon sticks, star anise, and nutmeg. There's even a project for your favorite green thumb, complete with gardening implements. Add a charming touch to a bird lover's front door with a wreath covered in birdseed. And for those who love to play, don't forget game night with wreaths that spotlight your family's favorite board games, or a Texas Hold 'Em wreath that's a sure bet to warm the heart of your favorite gambler.

Artist

Materials

- 2" circle punch
- 6" artist's mannequin
- 14" grapevine wreath
- Cardstock scraps: blue, green, orange, purple, red, yellow
- Colored pencils: 4–6
- Craft scissors
- Hot glue gun and glue sticks
- Inkpad: to match cardstock colors
- Masking tape
- No. 2 pencil
- Paint tubes (3)
- Paintbrushes (3 large, 3 small)
- Plastic wrap
- Ribbon: 2" black-and-white dotted grosgrain
- Ruler
- Spray paint: blue, red, yellow
- Wire cutters

Instructions

1. Using paper punch, create one circle of each cardstock color. Ink edges with coordinating colors. Hot glue circles to wreath in color wheel pattern.

2. Cover ferrule and bristles of large brushes with plastic wrap and masking tape and then spray various paint colors; let dry and then remove plastic wrap.

3. Adhere large brushes to right side of wreath with hot glue. Adhere small unpainted brushes on right side of large brushes.

4. Hot glue paint tubes and colored pencils onto left side of wreath.

time-saving tip

Any Pencil Will Do

If you don't have a ready supply of colored pencils, any brightly colored lead pencils will do. Just sharpen the pencils to different lengths. The colored leads will not be missed.

With all the bold colors of the Artist wreath, the black and white ribbon gives the eye a rest.

5. Tie 1 yard of ribbon into a simple bow and hot glue in place; trim ends.

6. Remove base from mannequin with wire cutters. Apply hot glue to metal shaft and insert into wreath. Position feet on grapevine and add hot glue for stability. Hot glue pencil in hands.

The handles of the paintbrushes are spray painted eye-catching primary colors that really "pop."

time-saving tip

Adapt a Hobby

This wreath could be easily altered for a rubber stamper. Just add rubber stamps and small inkpads to the array of art materials, since stampers use many of the same products as painters.

Game Day

Materials

- 12" x 14" foam wreath
- Cosmetic sponge
- Craft glue
- Craft scissors
- Foam brush
- Game pieces (32)
- Hot glue gun and glue sticks: low-temp
- Inkpad: brown
- Play money
- Ribbon: ½" black-and-white
- Ruler

Instructions

1. Apply craft glue to wreath with foam brush. Adhere play money to completely cover. Using cosmetic sponge, lightly rub brown ink directly on paper money to distress.

2. Hot glue game pieces to surface of wreath.

3. Tie 2 yards of ribbon into bow. Adhere to top of wreath with hot glue.

time-saving tip

Switch It Up

There's no need to use game pieces all from the same game. Here, pieces were culled from five different games to create the Game Day wreath.

Knitting

Materials

- 14" foam wreath
- Balls of yarn: small coordinating (3)
- Craft scissors: medium, small
- Hot glue gun and glue sticks: low-temp
- Knitted scarf
- Knitting needles (2 pairs)
- Measuring tape
- Ribbon: ½" sheer; 3" coordinating
- T-pins (about 30)

Instructions

1. Measure wreath circumference. Measure that distance plus 2" on scarf and apply strip of hot glue across scarf to prevent raveling. Cut scarf with medium-size scissors.

2. Pin scarf to wreath, stretching as needed, and wrap securely all the way around.

3. Wrap 2 yards of sheer ribbon around wreath; secure in place with T-pins.

4. Tie 3 yards of ribbon into florist bow at center top of wreath with coordinating ribbon. Tuck each pair of knitting needles on either side of bow.

5. Adhere yarn balls in curve of lower part of wreath; secure in place with T-pins.

6. Adhere small craft scissors with hot glue.

Baker

Materials

- 14" willow wreath
- Anise pods (10)
- Antiquing spray paint
- Cinnamon sticks (about 60)
- Craft scissors
- Hot glue gun and glue sticks
- Raffia: natural
- Ruler

Instructions

1. Spray willow wreath with antiquing spray paint; let dry.

2. Hot glue 6–7 cinnamon sticks to wreath to create the look of bundles. Wrap raffia around bundles, tying knot on top; trim 1" from knot. Repeat to cover wreath with cinnamon sticks.

3. Adhere anise pods to center of raffia knot with hot glue.

time-saving tip

Take it up a Notch

If you want to really pile on the embellishments, consider hot gluing measuring spoons or any other small kitchen utensils to this wreath.

Gardener's Delight

Materials

- ⅛" hole punch
- Adhesives: cellophane tape, glue dots
- Craft scissors
- Eyelet setting tools
- Eyelets (2)
- Inkpads: colors of your choice (3)
- Millinery flower stem
- Playing cards with decorative backs (6)
- Ribbon: ½" black-and-cream checked
- Rubber stamps: sea-themed (2)
- Ruler
- Seed packets (8)
- Shipping tag

Instructions

1. Punch holes in upper right and upper left corners of seed packets. Attach eyelets in seed packet that will serve as centerpiece.

2. To determine length of ribbon to cut, measure from hole to hole of punched packets, then multiply by 3 and cut. Wrap piece of tape around end of ribbon and use to thread through punched holes as shown; thread last packet so it will dangle.

3. Center packets, then tie both ends of ribbon to form circle.

4. Using glue dots in upper right and upper left corners of back of playing cards, attach one between each of the seed packets. Add more glue dots if needed to further stabilize.

5. Using rubber stamps and inkpads, stamp design onto shipping tag, then slip ribbons through hole in tag until tag reaches knot in ribbon. Tie into simple bow.

6. Slip millinery stem through shipping tag hole and make loop out of stem to hang wreath.

Texas Hold 'Em

Materials

- 12" particle board floral wreath form
- Dice (68)
- Hot glue gun and glue sticks
- Playing cards (3 boxes)
- Rubber toy dice (2)

Instructions

1. Arrange playing cards into "hands." Glue together using hot glue gun.

2. Attach to front of wreath form using hot glue gun, allowing about 1" space between each.

3. Fill in spaces by attaching a card turned face-down on backside of wreath form.

4. Randomly attach dice to inside edge area of wreath using hot glue gun.

5. Attach playing card boxes to backside of wreath base with hot glue.

6. Attach large rubber dice to bottom center inside edge of wreath with hot glue.

time-saving tip

Games People Play

Pieces from favorite games can make a fun and quick wreath, and are sure to please aficionados. Dominos, checkers, play money, board markers, and jigsaw puzzle pieces can be arranged symmetrically or in a random pattern and attached to a flat base with a hot glue gun.

Bird Lover

Materials

- 4" bird nest
- 12" foam wreath
- Birdseed
- Craft glue
- Craft scissors
- Floral wire
- Foam brush
- Hot glue gun and glue sticks: low-temp
- Ribbon: 2" blue-green
- Robin's eggs: plastic (3)
- Wire cutters

Instructions

1. Apply generous amount of craft glue to surface of wreath using foam brush; cover with birdseed. Repeat if necessary to achieve complete coverage.

2. Hot glue eggs to inside of nest. Tie large bow with 2 yards of ribbon; trim ends. Hot glue nest to center of bow. Attach bow to wreath using floral wire.

time-saving tip

It's Covered

Lay the glue-covered wreath in a box and sprinkle with birdseed to contain the excess and for a quicker clean up.

Little Boy Train

Materials

- 14" straw wreath
- Craft scissors
- Denim: worn jeans
- Floral wire
- Hot glue gun and glue sticks
- Painted vehicles and letters: balsa wood or chipboard
- Ribbon: 2" red-and-white checked
- Ruler
- Toy train track
- Washer and dryer
- Wire cutters

Instructions

1. Cut 2" strips of denim from worn jeans; machine wash and dry to fray edges. Wrap wreath with denim strips; hot glue to secure in place.

2. Hot glue train track, wooden shapes, and letters to front of wreath.

3. Tie 2 yards of ribbon into large bow; wire to top of wreath. Hot glue painted shape to center of bow.

Show its Age

New denim may be purchased from a fabric store, cut into lengths, and then washed for an aged appearance.

Contributors

Carlene Federer
Pages 24, 98

Carlene Federer is a mixed-media artist with a passion for all things shiny, rusty, sparkly, and vintage. She describes her personal style as "glitter-grunge." Carlene enjoys making many types and styles of arts and crafts, from scrapbooks and cards to shadowboxes, collages, and more. She is a frequent contributor to *Somerset Memories* and *Somerset Studio* magazines. She's also been featured in several idea books and magazines.

Carlene lives in Tempe, Arizona, with her husband and son. www.carlenefederer.blogspot.com.

Sunday Hendrickson
Pages 74, 92

Sunday Hendrickson is a well-known photo stylist, field editor, and producer. She has worked for a wide variety of clients including *Country Living*, *Home Magazine*, *Coastal Living*, *Family Circle*, *Woman's Day*, *Good Housekeeping*, and *Mary Engelbreit's Home Companion*, to name just a few. She obtained a bachelor of arts degree in Journalism from Pennsylvania State University and studied at the School of Visual Arts and Parsons School of Design, both in New York. Sunday has been the design director for *Ladies Home Journal*, art director for *Modern Bride* magazine, and creative director for Lovelace Publications.

Sunday lives in Los Angeles, California.

Cher Lashley
Pages 42, 82, 114

Cher Lashley is a self-taught artist and has owned an art supply and teaching shop. After becoming involved in oil painting and fine art, Cher participated in juried art shows and festivals as well as solo and group exhibitions in galleries throughout the Blue Ridge and Southern states as well as Arizona and Texas. She eventually opened her own gallery in St. Augustine, Florida. After closing her gallery's doors in 2003, Cher became obsessed with collage and altered art. She has taught workshops, designed gift lines, held gallery shows, and has published articles in several magazines.

Cher lives in Southern California.

Eileen Cannon Paulin

Pages 40, 60, 116

Ever since she can remember, Eileen Cannon Paulin has been fond of knitting, sewing, decoupaging, and just about any other handicraft she's seen as useful. She studied writing in college and has been able to combine her head with her heart's desires as a home décor magazine editor and now a book publisher. Eileen has appeared on HGTV and The Discovery Channel, and has been a frequent guest on "The Christopher Lowell Show." She is the author of "The Serene Home" (Sterling Publishing, © 2003) and "Decorating for the First Time" (Sterling Publishing, © 2003). Eileen is the founding girlfriend behind Red Lips 4 Courage Communications, a publishing services company that specializes in conceptualizing, writing, and producing hardcover books for women, about women.

Eileen lives in Southern California with her husband and two children.

Roxi Phillips

Pages 28, 34, 48, 50, 68, 70, 76, 88, 90, 94, 108, 112, 118, 120

Roxi Phillips is an award-winning paper and mixed-media artist who has dabbled in a wide variety of crafts throughout her life. Her eclectic style and diversity is shown in her work, from altered art projects to more traditional scrapbooking.

Roxi designs paper arts projects using mixed media and scrapbooking techniques for several companies including Krylon® and Tapestry by CR Gibson®. Her work is featured regularly in national magazines such as *Scrapbooking and Beyond*, *PaperCrafts*, and *PaperWorks* and crafting books including *Spray Paint Paper Crafts: Creative Fun with Krylon* (Sterling Publishing, © 2007).

Roxi and her family live in western Tennessee.

Angie Poll

Pages 78, 86

Angie Poll has been arranging wedding flowers for more than a decade. She trained under a local floral designer before starting her own floral business, Lakeview Bridal, specializing in fresh and silk flowers for weddings. Angie relishes the challenge of trying new and different floral styles as she designs for excited brides. She works from home and enjoys the flexibility that it gives her.

Angie lives with her husband and four children in Syracuse, Utah. www.lakeviewbridal.com.

Melody Thompson

Pages 36, 44, 52, 54, 56, 58, 62, 80, 96, 100

Melody Thompson blends her passion for flowers and whimsical design to create vibrant faux floral arrangements. A Texas Master Florist, she founded a successful Austin, Texas, floral boutique featuring personal and original floral designs for weddings and special events. Her designs have been showcased in several bridal publications and shows. Melody is the author of "Make It in Minutes: Faux Floral Arrangements" (Sterling Publishing, © 2007).

Melody's creative background includes home interior design, antique retail, special event planning, and cosmetics training and artistry.

Melody lives in Austin, Texas, with her husband, Bill, and their two furry children.

Candice Windham

Pages 30, 72, 104, 110

Graphic designer, altered artist, paper crafter, rubber stamp artist, painter, and teacher, Candice Windham's work has appeared in various books and publications, including magazines *Altered Arts* and the premier issue of *Make It Mine*. She is also a museum curator and designer, combining her love of history and art. She is represented by the Rivertown Gallery in downtown Memphis, Tennessee.

Candice lives in Brighton, Tennessee, with her husband, Larry, son Michael, and pups, Pete and Sam.

METRIC EQUIVALENCY CHARTS

inches to millimeters and centimeters
(mm-millimeters, cm-centimeters)

inches	mm	cm	inches	cm	inches	cm
⅛	3	0.3	9	22.9	30	76.2
¼	6	0.6	10	25.4	31	78.7
½	13	1.3	12	30.5	33	83.8
⅝	16	1.6	13	33.0	34	86.4
¾	19	1.9	14	35.6	35	88.9
⅞	22	2.2	15	38.1	36	91.4
1	25	2.5	16	40.6	37	94.0
1¼	32	3.2	17	43.2	38	96.5
1½	38	3.8	18	45.7	39	99.1
1¾	44	4.4	19	48.3	40	101.6
2	51	5.1	20	50.8	41	104.1
2½	64	6.4	21	53.3	42	106.7
3	76	7.6	22	55.9	43	109.2
3½	89	8.9	23	58.4	44	111.8
4	102	10.2	24	61.0	45	114.3
4½	114	11.4	25	63.5	46	116.8
5	127	12.7	26	66.0	47	119.4
6	152	15.2	27	68.6	48	121.9
7	178	17.8	28	71.1	49	124.5
8	203	20.3	29	73.7	50	127.0

yards to meters

yards	meters	yards	meters	yards	meters	yards	meters	yards	meters
⅛	0.11	2⅛	1.94	4⅛	3.77	6⅛	5.60	8⅛	7.43
¼	0.23	2¼	2.06	4¼	3.89	6¼	5.72	8¼	7.54
⅜	0.34	2⅜	2.17	4⅜	4.00	6⅜	5.83	8⅜	7.66
½	0.46	2½	2.29	4½	4.11	6½	5.94	8½	7.77
⅝	0.57	2⅝	2.40	4⅝	4.23	6⅝	6.06	8⅝	7.89
¾	0.69	2¾	2.51	4¾	4.34	6¾	6.17	8¾	8.00
⅞	0.80	2⅞	2.63	4⅞	4.46	6⅞	6.29	8⅞	8.12
1	0.91	3	2.74	5	4.57	7	6.40	9	8.23
1⅛	1.03	3⅛	2.86	5⅛	4.69	7⅛	6.52	9⅛	8.34
1¼	1.14	3¼	2.97	5¼	4.80	7¼	6.63	9¼	8.46
1⅜	1.26	3⅜	3.09	5⅜	4.91	7⅜	6.74	9⅜	8.57
1½	1.37	3½	3.20	5½	5.03	7½	6.86	9½	8.69
1⅝	1.49	3⅝	3.31	5⅝	5.14	7⅝	6.97	9⅝	8.80
1¾	1.60	3¾	3.43	5¾	5.26	7¾	7.09	9¾	8.92
1⅞	1.71	3⅞	3.54	5⅞	5.37	7⅞	7.20	9⅞	9.03
2	1.83	4	3.66	6	5.49	8	7.32	10	9.14

INDEX

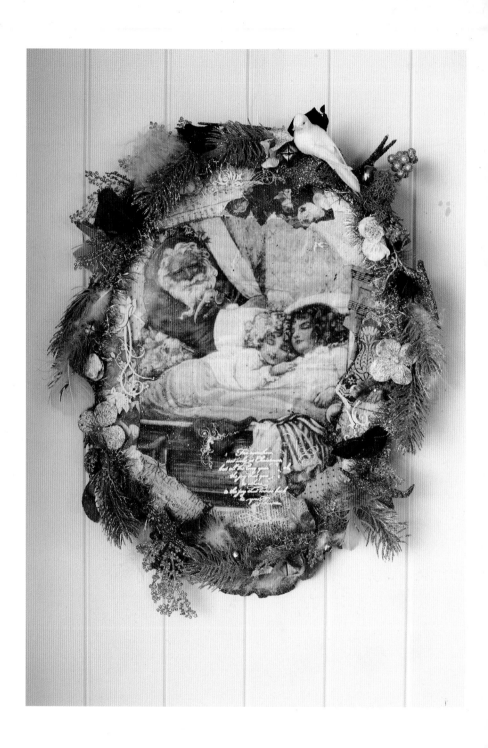